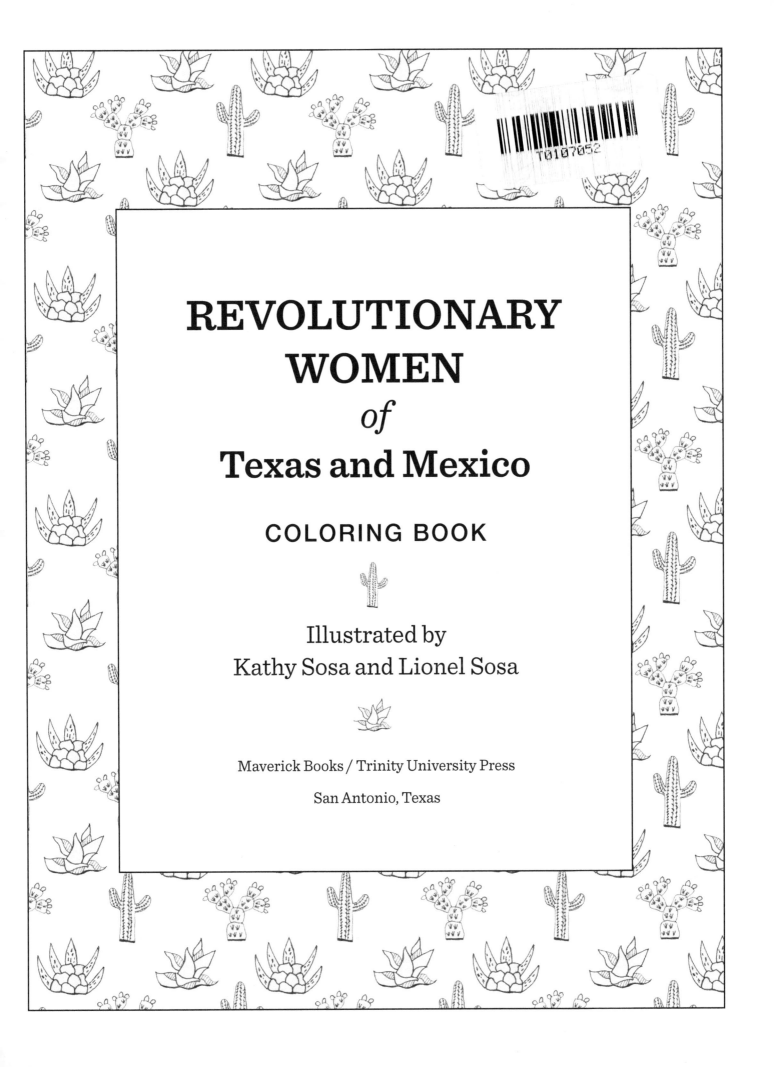

REVOLUTIONARY WOMEN

of

Texas and Mexico

COLORING BOOK

Illustrated by
Kathy Sosa and Lionel Sosa

Maverick Books / Trinity University Press

San Antonio, Texas

Published by Maverick Books
an imprint of Trinity University Press
San Antonio, Texas 78212

Book design by Anne Richmond Boston
Cover design by Erin Mayes
Cover illustration by Kathy Sosa

ISBN 978-1-59534-965-1 paperback

Trinity University Press strives to produce its books using methods and materials in an environmentally sensitive manner. We favor working with manufacturers that practice sustainable management of all natural resources, produce paper using recycled stock, and manage forests with the best possible practices for people, biodiversity, and sustainability. The press is a member of the Green Press Initiative, a nonprofit program dedicated to supporting publishers in their efforts to reduce their impacts on endangered forests, climate change, and forest dependent communities.

The paper used in this publication meets the minimum requirements of the American National Standard for Information Sciences—Permanence of Paper for Printed Library Materials, anSi 39.48-1992.

CIP data on file at the Library of Congress
24 23 22 21 | 5 4 3 2 1

A note from Kathy Sosa: Thank you to my coeditors Jennifer Speed and Ellen Riojas Clark for collaborating on the original book, and to Dolores Huerta and Norma Elia Cantú for lending their voices. Thank you to the contributors for writing the portraits: Cristina Deveraux Ramírez for Juana Belén Gutiérrez de Mendoza, Elena Poniatowska for Las Soldaderas, Lionel Sosa for Las Valientas, Lewis Fisher for the Preservationists, Jennifer Speed for Maria Concepción Acedvedo de la Llata, Laura Esquivel for La Malinche, the late Virgilio P. Elizondo for the Virgin of Guadalupe, Alicia Gaspar de Alba for Sor Juana Inés de la Cruz, Linda Hudson for Jane McManus Storm Cazneau, Sandra Cisneros for Teresa Urrea and Chavela Vargas, Teresa Van Hoy for Nahui Olin, Cynthia Orozco for Alice Dickerson Montemayor, Amalia Mesa-Bains for Frida Kahlo, Carmen Tafolla for Emma Tenayuca, Ellen Riojas Clark for Gloria Anzaldúa, Elaine Ayala for Genoveva Morales, and Hilary Klein for the Zapatistas. We hope the *Revolutionary Women of Texas and Mexico Coloring Book* becomes a springboard for sharing the histories and stories of more Latina women.

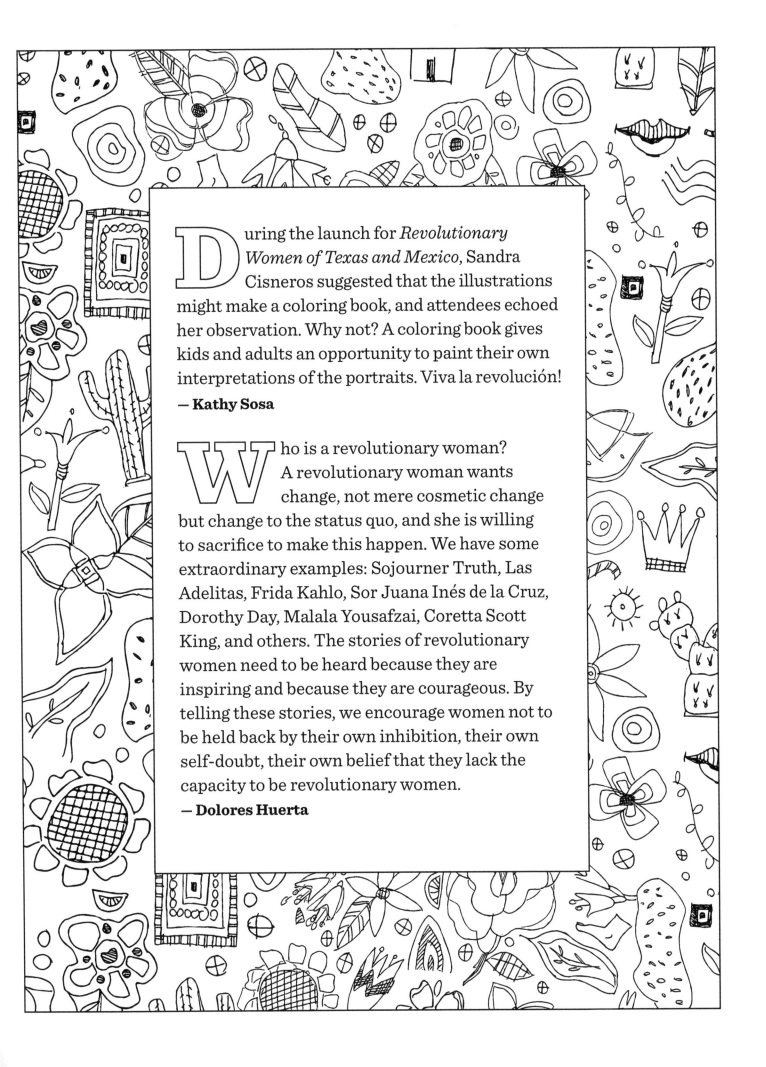

During the launch for *Revolutionary Women of Texas and Mexico*, Sandra Cisneros suggested that the illustrations might make a coloring book, and attendees echoed her observation. Why not? A coloring book gives kids and adults an opportunity to paint their own interpretations of the portraits. Viva la revolución!

— **Kathy Sosa**

Who is a revolutionary woman? A revolutionary woman wants change, not mere cosmetic change but change to the status quo, and she is willing to sacrifice to make this happen. We have some extraordinary examples: Sojourner Truth, Las Adelitas, Frida Kahlo, Sor Juana Inés de la Cruz, Dorothy Day, Malala Yousafzai, Coretta Scott King, and others. The stories of revolutionary women need to be heard because they are inspiring and because they are courageous. By telling these stories, we encourage women not to be held back by their own inhibition, their own self-doubt, their own belief that they lack the capacity to be revolutionary women.

— **Dolores Huerta**

Gloria Anzaldúa (b. Raymondville, Texas, 1942; d. Santa Cruz, California, 2004) was the child of farmworkers in South Texas and came to be a keen observer of social and cultural strife that touched race, ethnic, and gender relations in the world around her. First as a teacher and then as an academic and a writer, she articulated the compelling need to address sexual and ethnic multi-identities.

Gloria Anzaldúa

María Concepción Acevedo de la Llata
(b. Santiago de Querétaro, Mexico, 1891; d. Mexico City, Mexico, 1978), a Capuchin nun, was caught up in the violence connected with the Cristero War. Acevedo de la Llata, also known as Madre Conchita, was convicted as the intellectual author of and accomplice to the assassination of President Álvaro Obregón in 1928, but the trial was later judged to be a sham. Following her release from the Mexican penal colony of Islas Marías, Madre Conchita spent the rest of her life advocating for religious liberty and the rights of indigenous Mexicans, especially the Otomi people.

María Concepción Acevedo de la Llata

Jane McManus Storm Cazneau (b. Troy, New York, 1807; d. at sea, 1878), diplomat and adventurer, was the first woman appointed to the U.S. foreign service. She served during the Mexican-American War in the 1840s and conducted secret negotiations with the Mexican government. She also served as a war correspondent from Mexico and the Dominican Republic. Years earlier, though, she had thrown herself into the War of Texas Independence, giving money and weapons to the Texan cause.

Jane McManus Storm Cazneau

Sandra Cisneros (b. Chicago, Illinois, 1954) is an activist poet, fiction writer, essayist, educator, and artist whose award-winning books explore the lives of the working class. Her first book was the poetry collection *Bad Boys*, followed by the bestselling novel *The House on Mango Street*, which has been translated into multiple languages and utilized in school curricula around the world. The child of Mexican parents and sister to six brothers, Cisneros has been honored with a MacArthur Fellowship, the Texas Medal of the Arts, and a National Medal of Arts.

Sandra Cisneros

Ellen Riojas Clark (b. San Antonio, Texas, 1941) has dedicated her life to education and advocacy for equity and social justice for the Latino community by championing its arts and culture. She has written a book about tamales and is working on another on the history and types of pan dulce, and her work as cultural director of the PBS program *Maya and Miguel* has touched many lives. Her decades of distinguished research as a scholar of bilingual-bicultural studies will be honored with a named chair at the University of Texas at San Antonio—the first chaired position in the United States named for a Latina.

Ellen Riojas Clark

Laura Esquivel (b. Mexico City, Mexico, 1950) is a Mexican novelist, screenwriter, and politician. She became a storyteller by writing plays for her kindergarten students and scripts for children's television programs. She writes about topics often associated with women, like food, the kitchen, and love, in a unique way. Her first novel, the bestseller *Like Water for Chocolate*, takes the form of a cookbook. Esquivel was elected as federal representative for the Morena Party, and she has served as the head of the Mexico City Cultural Committee and on her party's committees for the environment and for science and technology.

¡Viva La Morena!

Laura Esquivel

The **Virgin of Guadalupe**, saint and cultural icon, first appeared to an Indian peasant in 1531 at the Hill of Tepeyac in Mexico City. The Virgin has been a malleable symbol for centuries, but her image as the patroness of revolutionaries and others who fight oppression has become especially powerful since the War of Mexican Independence and the Mexican Revolution.

Virgin of Guadalupe

Juana Belén Gutiérrez de Mendoza (b. San Juan del Río, Durango, Mexico, 1875; d. Michoacán/ Mexico City, Mexico, 1942), a journalist and militant, began her government protests while a young miner's wife in Coahuila. She sent essays to opposition newspapers in protest of the horrible living and working conditions for miners, angering both Porfirio Díaz and the powerful mining company owners. Later she endured multiple arrests not only for her newspapers, like *Vésper: Justicia y libertad* (which she printed as well), but also for her role in a military insurgency that tried to bring Francisco Madero to power. After the war she fought to bring about a social and economic revolution for Mexico's poorest citizens.

Juana Belén Gutiérrez de Mendoza

Astrid Hadad (b. Chetumal, Quintana Roo, Mexico, 1957) is a Mexican actress and vocalist whose performances in elaborate, outrageous costumes poke fun at human behavior, politics, and cultural values. She has produced more than ten albums and twenty-five shows and has appeared on Mexican soap operas. She studied political science at the National Autonomous University of Mexico but discovered that with theater, she could make people think about politics through her performing and singing.

PECADORA

Astrid Hadad

Dolores Huerta (b. Dawson, New Mexico, 1930) is a civil rights activist and U.S. labor leader. She cofounded the National Farmworkers Association, now known as United Farm Workers, with César E. Chávez, and in 2002 founded the Dolores Huerta Foundation, which creates leadership opportunities for community organizing, civic engagement, and policy advocacy. She has received the Presidential Eleanor Roosevelt Award for Human Rights, the Presidential Medal of Freedom, and the Radcliffe Medal.

Dolores Huerta

Sor Juana Inés de la Cruz (b. Mexico City, Mexico, 1648; d. Mexico City, 1695), colonial Mexico's luminary intellectual and poet, resisted church censorship of her writings. This was exceedingly difficult because the Catholic Church in colonial Mexico, through the auspices of the Holy Office of the Inquisition, had discretion over every aspect of religious life and any matter pertaining to morals. Even as Sor Juana gave evidence of complying with the Inquisition as a cloistered nun, she actively resisted its efforts to control her spirituality and intellectual creativity.

Sor Juana Inés de la Cruz

Frida Kahlo (b. Coyoacán, Mexico City, Mexico, 1907; d. Coyoacán, 1954) initiated an artistic revolution in both subject matter and expressions of the body and suffering. She profoundly identified with the Mexican Revolution for the ways it had disrupted the nation. Painting became a vehicle for expressing the magnitude of suffering that both Kahlo and the nation endured—the nation from conquest and the violence of war, and herself from polio and a catastrophic accident. It was also a means of bringing together Mexico's broken pieces in art.

Frida Kahlo

Malinalli, or Malintzín (b. Yucatán, Mexico, ca. 1500; d. Mexico City, Mexico, ca. 1529), as a young girl was traded to be a slave to Hernán Cortés following his defeat of a Mayan tribe near Tabasco. She served as Cortés's translator and an emissary as he made his way toward Mexico City and later bore two children with him. More frequently known as La Malinche, she is a highly contested figure in Mexican history, sometimes faulted for facilitating the Mexican conquest at the side of Cortés and other times honored as a true soldier and mother of the Mexican people.

Malinalli

Alice Dickerson Montemayor (b. Laredo, Texas, 1904; d. Laredo, 1989) was a LULAC (League of United Latin American Citizens) activist and social worker. In her twenties she attacked LULAC's machismo culture and gender discrimination, initiating a revolution that broke down its barriers to female leadership. As a social worker in 1930s and 1940s South Texas, she took on racial and ethnic discrimination. When sheriffs and judges in Cotulla prevented Mexican American families from applying for services they were entitled to, she set up her operation on the courthouse lawn with a bodyguard supplied by the state. Her efficiency and determination won over local officials, who became her allies in providing equal access to state services.

Alice Dickerson Montemayor

Educational activist **Genoveva Morales** (b. Uvalde, Texas, 1928) was the lead plaintiff in a watershed federal lawsuit that eroded discriminatory practices in public schools. She challenged discrimination in schools in Uvalde, Texas, in 1970 and persisted in the lawsuit for nearly forty years. In doing so, she ended institutionalized educational discrimination in Uvalde and has given thousands of Mexican American students there and elsewhere equal access to education under the law.

Genoveva Morales

Nahui Olin (b. Mexico City, Mexico, 1893; d. Mexico City, 1978), an artist and writer, used her talent in the 1920s to express her intellect and to break down gender barriers at a time when Mexican women were severely constrained by law and social custom. A painter and photographer who organized her own shows, Olin invaded an artistic realm dominated by men, making it possible for other women, like Frida Kahlo, to explore their art without limitation.

Nahui Olin

Preservationists The preservation movement west of the Mississippi was born in San Antonio, Texas, in the early decades of the twentieth century, gaining momentum when a group of courageous women turned their wills to conserving historic sites, cultural landmarks, and natural habitats. Their influence would lead to the 1924 establishment of the San Antonio Conservation Society, and in the decades since, many preservationists, mostly women, have continued the cause. Today the missions they fought to save have earned UNESCO World Heritage Site designations, and the city is renowned for protecting its historic assets. Adina De Zavala, teacher and granddaughter of Lorenzo de Zavala; Emily Edwards, artist, author, and friend of Diego Rivera; and Rena Maverick Green were three of the movement's earliest leaders.

Preservationists

Soldaderas The adelita (activist) or *soldadera* (soldier) of the Mexican Revolution is in some ways hard to characterize, for her image in life and in art is often hard to separate. Usually lacking supply and medical units, Mexican armies were utterly dependent on soldaderas—women hired by or related to soldiers—as their quartermasters. Soldaderas, sometimes with children in tow, followed the troops on foot, set up camp, foraged for food and firewood, washed and mended the soldiers' clothing, tended the wounded, and even buried the dead. In life and in song, soldaderas became the romanticized sweethearts of and helpmates to their soldiers as valentinas (brave ones) and adelitas.

Soldaderas

In 1938 labor organizer **Emma Tenayuca** (b. San Antonio, Texas, 1916; d. San Antonio, 1989) led a successful strike of twelve thousand pecan shellers in San Antonio, nearly all of them Mexican American women and children. She was eventually forced to leave San Antonio for her work as a labor, community, and political organizer. She returned twenty years later to teach children basic skills like reading and to ensure that they continued on the path of social and political revolution for Mexican Americans in Texas.

Emma Tenayuca

Teresa Urrea (b. Ocoroni, Sinaloa, Mexico, 1873; d. Clifton, Arizona, 1906), a healer and later a patroness of Indians in northern Mexico, is an icon of borderlands culture. She became a reluctant revolutionary when Indians fighting Porfirio Díaz came to believe that she would protect them from death or injury in battle. Because insurgents called her their saint, Díaz blamed her for inciting rebellion, exiled her, and tried to have her killed. In the century since her death, her image as a political and cultural revolutionary has been fashioned under many guises.

Teresa Urrea

Valientas The Mexican Revolution wreaked havoc on families throughout the country. Husbands and fathers disappeared, victims of conscription, casualties of battle, or consumed by a desire for adventure. The women who accompanied their men to war gained notoriety as *soldaderas*, actively functioning as supply lines and joining the fight. But waves of their sisters chose another path: to escape war ravaged Mexico for los Estados Unidos. Many had small children in tow. Many settled in Texas, starting new lives from nothing. Their descendants became leaders in cities like San Antonio, transforming communities into hubs of Latino culture.Unlike the soldaderas, this group's role in history has gone virtually unnoticed. We will christen this group with the name they deserve: *las valientas* (the brave ones).

Valientas

Isabel Vargas Lizano (b. San Joaquín de Flores, Costa Rica, 1919; d. Cuernavaca, Mexico, 2012) is better known as the singer Chavela Vargas, who claimed Mexico as her artistic birthplace and upended strict gender norms in mid-twentieth-century Mexico by dressing as a man and singing her renditions of rancheras. Pedro Almodóvar called her *la voz aspera de la ternura*, or the rough voice of tenderness. The Latin Academy of Recording Arts and Sciences presented Vargas with a Latin Grammy and a Lifetime Achievement Award. Latin American music was greatly influenced by her interpretations of many traditional genres and songs.

Isabel Vargas Lizano

Zapatistas   Indigenous peasant women from the southern Mexican state of Chiapas have helped lead the Zapatista movement for more than three decades, inspiring people worldwide with their courage. The movement stepped onto the stage on January 1, 1994, with a brief armed uprising; today it is more broadly known as a struggle for land and indigenous rights. Women have participated alongside men as insurgents, political leaders, healers, and educators. They have catalyzed dramatic changes in gender roles and continue to offer a vision of alternatives to global capitalism.

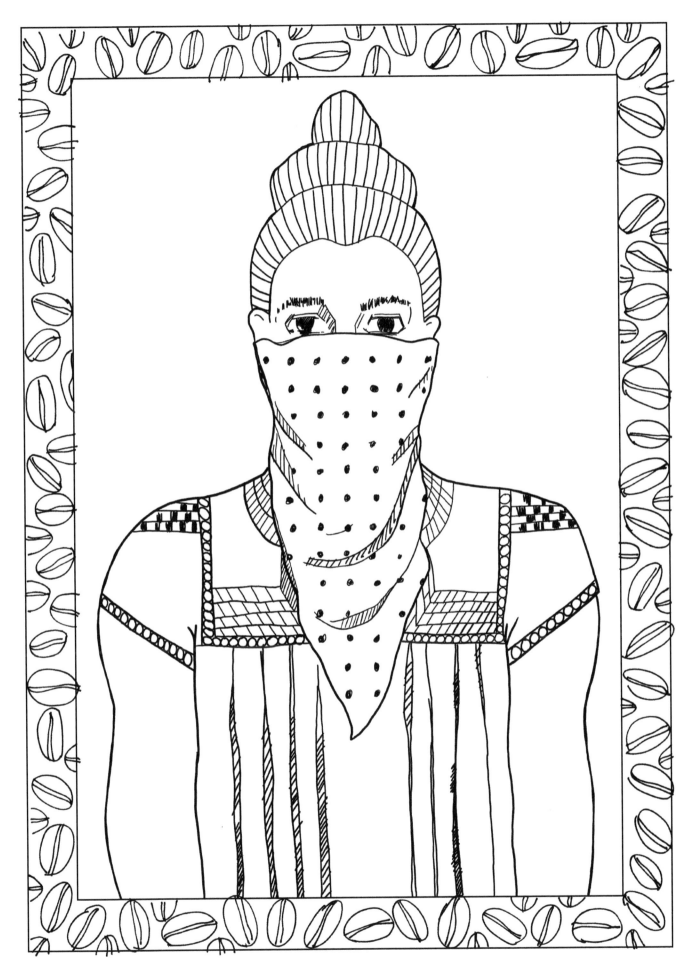

Zapatistas

Women often say that they are not trying to make history, they are just trying to make a change. But that's how you make history. Learn more about these revolutionary women in the book that inspired the coloring book, *Revolutionary Women of Texas and Mexico: Portraits of Soldaderas, Saints, and Subversives*.

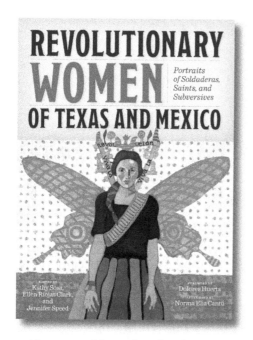

Read the stories of eighteen famous women across three time periods including the Virgin of Guadalupe, La Malinche, Frida Kahlo, and Emma Tenayuca as told by luminaries Sandra Cisneros, Laura Esquivel, Elena Poniatowska, and others. Also included are a capsule summary of the Mexican Revolution and inspiring essays by civil rights activist Dolores Huerta and writer Norma Elia Cantú on what makes women revolutionary.

Available at neighborhood and online bookstores or at tupress.org.

CPSIA information can be obtained
at www.ICGtesting.com
Printed in the USA
JSHW051205201121
20642JS00007B/14